Family Life Illustrated

For MEN

RONNIE FLOYD

Family Life Illustrated

For MEN

RONNIE FLOYD

New Leaf Press

Family Life Illustrated for Men

First printing: November 2004

ISBN: 0-89221-584-4
Library of Congress Number: 2004106954

Cover concept by Left Coast Design, Portland, OR

All sidebar statistics have been provided by: The Barna Group Online, 1957 Eastman Ave Ste B, Ventura, CA 93003. (www.barna.org/FlexPage.aspx?Page=Topic&TopicID=21)

Printed in the United States of America

Please visit our website for other great titles:
www.newleafpress.net

For information regarding author interviews, please contact the publicity department at (870) 438-5288.

CONTENTS

Introduction: Just for Men 6

1. Men Are Different Than Women 10

2. Jesus, the Man's Man 16

3. Why Do We Struggle? 24

4. Seven Principles for Significance, Part I 42

5. Seven Principles for Significance, Part II 58

6. Wanted: Battlefield Commanders 78

Just For Men

THE U.S. Marine Corps is not the only one looking for a few good men. So is God.

> I looked for a man among them who would build up the wall and stand before me in the gap on behalf of the land so I would not have to destroy it, but I found none (Ezek. 22:30).

In days gone by, God diligently searched Israel for a godly man with a few key characteristics:

- A man who knew and identified with his fellow citizens

- A man who would do the hard work of building

- A man who would take a stand

- A man who would live boldly before the Lord

It really doesn't sound like too much to ask for, does it? And yet, search as He might with His all-seeing eyes, God never found such a man. And because He didn't, His people endured 70 years of hard captivity in a foreign land.

Now, fast forward about 27 centuries. If God were still looking for that man to build walls and stand in the gap, what would He find? I'm not sure, but I think He'd say that a good man is *still* hard to find.

But things don't have to stay that way. The situation really can get better! In fact, that's the reason for this little book.

In *Men Illustrated*, I'm not so much searching for a good man as I am challenging Christian men to become the good men God already has equipped them to be. Consider this slim volume a trumpet blast to wake up the sleepy troops, get them moving, and get busy doing what God has called them to do.

That being the case, this is *not* a balanced book. It does not try to give a nuanced case for anything. Rather, it's a reveille call — short, to the point, and directed at a single group: Christian men. You won't find here a balanced presentation of the distinct roles found in a healthy family. No. This is a book for men, to men, by a man. And it has basically a single message.

It's time to step it up, men. It's time to leave behind the excuses and become the spiritual leaders God intends for us to be. In fact, it's past time.

That's it.

Epperson's law: When a man says it's a silly, childish game, it's probably something his wife can beat him at.

Don Epperson, quoted by Bill Gold in Washington Post, Reader's Digest, January, 1980.

Give us clear vision that

we may know where to stand

and what to stand for, because

unless we stand for something,

we shall fall for anything.

– *Peter Marshall*

Chapter 1

Men Are Different Than Women

A SHORT time ago we dubbed a man who works at our church a "great scholar" for the insightful comment he made in a staff meeting: "Men are different than women."

You know, I think he just might have something there.

Men *are* different from women, even though our culture likes to deny it, oppose it, and even vilify it. The crucial differences between the sexes remain, however, as my daughter-in-law, Kate, reminded me a few months ago. It was she who sent me the following (tongue-firmly-in-cheek) male/female comparison:

Boy, Godzilla, Peanut Head, and Scrappy.

- Concerning eating out: When the bill arrives, Mike, Charlie, Bob, and John will each throw in $20, even though the bill comes to only $32.50; none of them will have anything smaller, and none will actually admit they want change back. When the women get their bill, out come the pocket calculators.

- Concerning money: A man will pay two dollars for a one-dollar item that he wants. A woman will pay one dollar for a two-dollar item that she doesn't want.

Men Versus Women — Round One

- Concerning nicknames: If Laura, Susan, Debra, and Rose go out to lunch, they will call each other Laura, Susan, Debra, and Rose. If Mike, Charlie, Bob, and John go out, they will affectionately refer to each other as Fat

- Concerning bathrooms: A man has six items in his bathroom: a toothbrush, shaving cream, razor, a bar of soap, and a towel from the Holiday Inn. The average number of items in the typical woman's bathroom is 337, most of which a man could not identify.

- Concerning arguments: A woman has the last word in any argument; anything a man says after that is the beginning of a new argument.

- Concerning cats: Women love cats. Men say they love cats, but when women are not looking, men kick cats.

- Concerning the future: A woman worries about the future until she gets a husband. A man never worries about the future until he gets a wife.

- Concerning success: a successful man is one who makes more money than his wife can spend. A successful woman is one who can find such a man.

- Concerning marriage: A woman marries a man expecting he will change, but he doesn't. A man marries a woman expecting she won't change, and she does.

- Concerning dressing up: A woman will dress up to go shopping, water the plants, empty the garbage, answer the phone, read a book, and get the mail. A man will dress up for weddings and funerals.

- Concerning physical appearance: Men wake up as good-looking as they did when they went to bed. Women somehow deteriorate during the night.

- Concerning off-spring: A woman knows all about her children; she knows about dentist appointments and romances, best friends, favorite foods, secret fears, and hopes and dreams. A man is vaguely aware of some short people living in his house.

A successful man is one who makes more money than his wife can spend.

And here's the thought for the day:

- Any married man should forget his mistakes; there is no use in two people remembering the same thing.

I laughed out loud when I read what Kate sent me. But beyond the jokes and funny observations, men and women really *are* different, and those differences concern far more than appearance or plumbing. Many male/female differences go to the heart of what it means to be a man or a woman — and we ignore or trample them at our own peril.

This little book focuses exclusively on the masculine side of the ledger and unapologetically calls men to remember who they really are and then to act on that knowledge. And just who are men? What is a man really like?

In my opinion, no better example exists than Jesus Christ himself.

A woman has the last word in any argument; anything a man says after that is the beginning of a new argument.

FIVE MAJOR NEEDS OF . . .

WOMEN

1) Affection

2) Conversation

3) Honesty and openness

4) Financial support

5) Family commitment

MEN

1) Sexual fulfillment

2) Recreational companionship

3) An attractive spouse

4) Domestic support

5) Admiration

"His Needs, Her Needs," quoted in C. Swindoll,
The Grace Awakening, Word, 1990, p. 256.

Chapter 2

Jesus, the Man's Man

BEYOND all question, Jesus Christ was "different than a woman." Our Lord was a man's man. If you're looking for a picture of true masculinity, just observe Jesus Christ and his life as described in the Gospels. There you'll find a bold portrait of genuine manhood.

Jesus began his public ministry by marching alone into the wilderness, where he stayed 40 days without eating anything. I've seen that wilderness, with its venomous snakes and biting scorpions and other unpleasant little creatures — you don't want to hang around out there for 40 days! But Jesus did. Why? Because that's where the Spirit led Him, and Jesus made it His habit

to go wherever the Spirit directed, say whatever the Spirit prompted, and do whatever the Spirit instructed (Luke 4:1).

And why did the Spirit lead Jesus into the wilderness? The Bible tells us that God sent Jesus into the desert for a very specific purpose: "to be tempted by the devil" (Matt. 4:1). The Lord of the universe wanted to show us how a man's man confronts and overcomes the worst temptations that Satan can throw at human beings. Jesus refused to "cheat" during this ordeal by relying on the omnipotence rightfully His as the Son of God, but instead depended completely upon the Holy Spirit and the Word of God to give Him the strength He needed to defeat Satan. Did it cost Him? You bet! The Scripture says that the devil's ferocious assault caused Jesus a lot of "suffering," but it also says that's why Jesus "is able to help those who are being tempted" (Heb. 2:18). Think of it: God sent Jesus into the desert to suffer terrible temptation, just to give us the help we need! In that desolate wilderness, Satan threw everything he had against Jesus — every temptation known to man — and yet Jesus came through the battle victorious ("without sin," in the Bible's terms) (Heb. 4:15). Jesus wrestled with the devil and won.

That's a man's man.

Throughout his public ministry, Jesus challenged and took on the ugly and powerful forces of the evil one. No one had ever seen anything like it — including the demonic hordes themselves. One day a satanic confrontation occurred during a Jewish worship service. A demon that had taken possession of a man cried out through the man's tortured voice, "What do you want with us, Jesus of Nazareth? Have you come to destroy us? I know who you are — the Holy One of God!"

Jesus had no time for the underlings of Satan or their dirty tricks. He knew how to confront and overcome the mafia of the underworld and so he commanded the demon, "Be quiet! Come out of him!" Immediately the demon threw the man down in front of everyone in the synagogue — but Luke adds

Jesus courageously fought against an intransigent, institutional bureaucracy and never backed down . . .

that "the demon . . . came out without injuring him" (Luke 4:33–35).

Only a man's man could do something like that.

Jesus spent most of His days pouring himself out in ministry to the poor, the brokenhearted, and the diseased. Jesus continually dealt with tough people in spiritual, physical, and emotional bond-age. Everywhere He went, Jesus cast His vision of the kingdom of God. As an entrepreneur, He created something out of nothing. He gave His life to a single, consuming mission. He traveled by foot around ancient Palestine with 12 often contentious men, continually speaking to thousands of needy Isra-elites, exhausting himself physically for the cause.

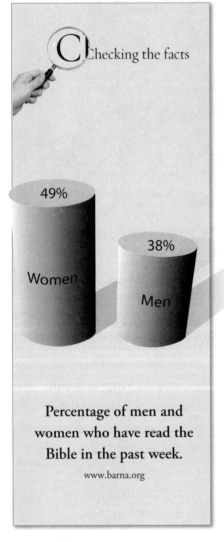

Checking the facts

49%
Women

38%
Men

Percentage of men and women who have read the Bible in the past week.

www.barna.org

That's a man's man.

Jesus courageously fought against an intransigent, institutional bureaucracy and never backed down, even when his opponents threatened his life. Jesus dealt effectively with powerful enemies and never winced at their barks or caved in to their attempted intimidation.

That's a man's man.

Jesus followed a deliberate strategy to take the world. He led a disciplined life, rising early in the morning to pray. On many occasions He prayed all night.

That's a man's man.

Jesus was a truth teller, calling it like it really is. He spoke up when dangerous men told Him to keep quiet and He kept quiet when powerful men told Him to speak up. He knew when He needed to use gentle words and He knew when He needed to use stinging words, and He never hesitated to speak exactly the right thing at exactly the right moment.

That's a man's man.

Jesus never shrank from accepting the very cruel death that He knew awaited Him. Arrested, beaten, and tried unfairly, yet able to destroy all His persecutors, He restrained himself — the hallmark of a truly great man. One day at high noon at the OK corral in hell, Jesus went nose to nose with the grave and with the devil — and won!

That's a man's man, to the nth degree.

> *Jesus never shrank from accepting the very cruel death that He knew awaited Him.*

No one, before or since, has exemplified true, strong, absolute masculinity, as thoroughly did Jesus Christ. Do you want to know how a real man acts? Do you want to see genuine masculinity on display? Do you want to observe the ultimate in true manhood? Then carefully watch Jesus Christ in action.

But I'd like to take it a step further than this. We really should, for the need of the hour requires it. Our task is not merely to get a good idea of what true masculinity involves, but for every Christian male to step up and become the kind of man that Jesus Christ exemplified.

And we can't wait any longer.

So enough of the excuses. Enough of the waffling. Enough of the cowering. It's time for all of us — every man who calls Jesus Christ his Lord — to stand up and eagerly partner with the Holy Spirit in becoming strong, masculine believers who more and more resemble Jesus Christ (2 Cor. 3:18).

This is the kind of man that each one of us absolutely has to become in our homes.

And yet, unfortunately, many of us hesitate. We hold back. We hang our heads, kick a stone along the sidewalk, and slowly amble on down the block.

Why? What makes us react like this? That's what I want to take a look at in the next chapter. Because I believe that if we can get some insight into what keeps us back, maybe we can finally start moving forward.

The little troubles and worries

of life may be as stumbling

blocks in our way, or we may

make them stepping-stones

to a nobler character and to

Heaven. Troubles are often the

tools by which God fashions us

for better things.

– Henry Ward Beecher

Chapter 3

Why Do We Struggle?

LET me ask you a question. Do you see yourself as a strong man? Do you picture yourself as the kind of man's man that Jesus was? If not, why not? Why do you struggle to see yourself as the kind of man God created you to be?

The truth is, all of us struggle with our masculinity at some point. And I believe there are at least five forces that cause us the most trouble.

The Feminization of the American Male

The number-one reason why many of us men have such a hard time picturing ourselves as strong is that our culture has feminized the male gender. Many forces have tried to neutralize a man's masculinity and

subsequently to emasculate his leadership responsibility. Everywhere you go in America, you see environments dominated by women. Why? Because too many men are unwilling to step up and live out their true masculinity.

Many men become shrinking violets when it comes to leadership because they grew up in families where Dad died or fled or otherwise remained absent. Oh, he may have been physically present in the home, but he was never there emotionally. Or he was barely there physically because he worked his life away. Either way, you had to go to Mom to get anything done. She became the "power heavy" in the family because she, at least, was willing to make decisions — something her passive husband refused to do.

Have you heard of the new term, "metrosexual"? It refers to a heterosexual male in touch with his feminine side. Let me tell you something: God doesn't want you to become a metrosexual. God has designed you to be a masculine man. Men don't need to get in touch with their feminine side. Do you know why? *They don't have one!* The Bible nowhere says men have a feminine

> *God didn't design you to think like a woman.*

side. Tender? Sure. Gentle? Absolutely. Caring? No question. But you don't need to get in touch with some imaginary "feminine side" to access such godly traits; rather, you need only to tap into your true, biblical masculinity. You have only to emulate the man's man, Jesus Christ.

No man needs to think like a woman. God didn't design you to think like a

woman. God designed you to be a man, unique in the eyes of God.

So what if society pictures us men as dumb? Let me set it straight, just for the record: I would rather be a dumb but masculine man, than a smart but feminine man. And so I am doing what I can to counteract the feminization of the male gender.

We Forfeit the Future for the Immediate

Men all across this country cave in to their media-inflamed desires or to their fear of conflict and so refuse to think through how their actions today will impact their lives tomorrow. Everything in our culture shouts, "Get it now! Do it now! Buy it now! Enjoy it now!" We live in an immediate culture — but God doesn't want us to forfeit the future for the immediate.

I know many men who feel that as long as they provide for their family, they're fulfilling their biblical responsibility. Their entire identity comes from being a provider. And that means once they've provided for the physical needs of their family, they "check out." Once they feel satisfied they've done their duty — taking care of the immediate — they slip into automatic mode and refuse to see what other leadership roles might be required of them to rear a healthy, maturing family — taking care of the future.

But do we really think that providing for physical needs is our only God-given role in the family? Do we really think that if we supply the home, the car, the food, and the clothes, that we can call ourselves successful men? If that's what we think, we're fooling ourselves. While most men I know are good providers most of the time, many of us are very poor at providing masculine, spiritual leadership in the home. And when we provide materially but fail to provide spiritually, we are forfeiting the future for the immediate.

Let me give just one example. It amazes me how many men will choose peace in the home at any price. They probably know that this behavior needs to be confronted or that habit has to be challenged, but they loathe the conflict more than they desire a godly home. So it's almost as if they enter an emotional vacuum when they get home after a hard day's work. "I don't want any more of this!" they shout as soon as the potential for some conflict erupts. "I had this all day long, and I don't need it here at home!" So they quash the conflict, but never tackle it head-on as any good spiritual leader must.

Listen, our homes don't need peace at any price; sometimes they *need* a controlled explosion, especially if a man has neglected to step up and act like a man. I know some husbands who could use a grenade down their shorts. They desperately need something to rouse their masculinity and bring some much-needed direction to their out-of-control wives. I know some fathers who could use a bomb under their easy chair. They need to start acting like a man and get control of their kids. And why aren't they willing to take control and assume their God-given leadership role? Because they want current "peace" more than they want long-term family health — and in so doing,

Many men remind me of the dog who gives the once-over to a skunk. He knows he could whip that skunk — he's just not sure it's worth it.

they forfeit the future for the immediate.

A lot of men know they need to get their households under control. They know they need to become the spiritual leaders of their homes — but they don't do it, because they're just not sure it's worth the battle. And so they forfeit the future for the immediate.

We Make Ourselves Slaves to Machines, Organizations, and Fantasies

Most men are suckers for gadgets. We drool over the latest cell phones, salivate over the newest computers, and slobber over the hottest "must have" piece of high-tech equipment. We put ourselves at the beck and call of technology, 24-7. We're generally terrible about becoming slaves to machines.

Others among us get totally wrapped up in health clubs or service organizations or corporate structures or lodges or other time-consuming groups. Whether we like the secret handshakes or the opportunity to hobnob with movers and shakers or the chance to impress onlookers, we let a good thing become a consuming thing, and our families suffer for it. It is a deadly mistake to give away your life in exchange for becoming a slave to an organization.

Still others among us find ourselves in bondage to various fantasies. Some men shackle themselves in the chains of a persistent fantasy about building their own corporate empire. Others choose freedom-stealing fantasies involving recreational activities, or a bigger house, or an alternate life, or practically anything else. But the most obvious (and perhaps widespread) of these fantasies concerns firm, shapely bodies in various stages of undress. Why do we nurture such destructive fantasies? Because we permit ourselves to feel discontented most of the time.

A recent survey found that more than 90 percent of a group of 550 Christian men named lust, pornography, or sexual fantasy as the number one reason for their spiritual disconnection.[1] Listen to me, men: you cannot walk with God if lust dominates your mind. You will spiritually disconnect if you immerse yourself in a pornographic scene, whether it be on the Internet or in magazines or videos or movies, or even if you allow yourself to fantasize about women in the office or in your neighborhood.

> *Listen to me, men: you cannot walk with God if lust dominates your mind.*

Of course, you'll always be able to find people like Professor Simon Blackburn, one of England's "most highly regarded philosophers," who recently published a book with Oxford University Press that claims lust is good for you.[2] Blackburn wants lust to be "reclaimed for humanity" and says, "The task I set myself is to lift it from the category of sin to that of virtue." Lust is fun, he says; just because it can get out of hand, doesn't mean it should be condemned. Best it should flow freely. He blames the bad reputation of lust on "old men of the desert" like St. Augustine and St. Thomas Aquinas.

If he's right, however, it's hard to see how men from the fourth century A.D. (and later) managed to influence godly men from the first century A.D., such as St. Paul, St. Peter, and St. John, all of who roundly condemned lust (Col. 3:5; 1 Pet. 4:3; 1 John 2:16). And it's even more difficult to see how these "old men of the desert" got Jesus Christ to go along with their silly ideas, since Jesus is the one who said, centuries before these "old men of the desert" were even born, "But I tell you that anyone who looks at a woman lustfully has already committed adultery with her in his heart" (Matt. 5:28).

When we willingly allow machines, organizations, and fantasies to hijack our lives, it's very difficult for us to fully experience genuine masculinity.

It doesn't look to me as though he meant it as a compliment.

When we willingly allow machines, organizations, and fantasies to hijack our lives, it's very difficult for us to fully experience genuine masculinity. When we become the willing slaves of these poor substitutes, our manhood takes a beating — and so do our families.

We Fail to Pay the Price to Get Equipped

Too many of us men remain unteachable about spiritual things; we simply are not willing to pay the price to get equipped for a life of genuine manhood. Many of us, for example, don't want to hear instructions or receive guidance about family matters because we determined years ago that what we learned from our peers or from the bathroom wall would do us just fine. God help us!

We men tend to think we know it all. We think we've heard it all. So we dismiss the idea that someone really might have something worthwhile to tell us. But do you know our real problem? It's not, of course, that we really know what we say we know. Rather, it's that we're too occupied with playing our own games — whether in the business world or in our recreational lives — to take the time to get equipped. We're too busy playing around with fun-but-temporary stuff to give our attention to harder-but-eternal stuff. We men generally have a hard time paying the price to get equipped.

Now, stop that nonsense for a moment and listen to me. Are you willing to get equipped to be everything God wants you to be as a man? Are you willing to pay the price to say goodbye to the TV for a few hours to put yourself under the instruction of the Word of God? Or are you going to wait until your family's gone and your kids are gone and you feel a total sense of restlessness ripping up your life? Will you wait until you feel miserable and totally discontented? Will you wait until your wife feels miserable, your kids feel miserable, and even your dog feels miserable? What's it going to take?

Millions of dead men already have proven that you can "have it all" and still feel empty, lonely, utterly foolish, and absolutely miserable. Affluence alone never succeeds in the long haul.

I wonder — do you really want to be a man? Do you honestly want to follow in the strong and masculine footsteps of Jesus Christ? If so, you have no choice but to pay the price to get equipped.

We Do Not Understand Our True Identity as Men

Gordon Dalbey, the author of *Healing the Masculine Soul*, gets to the root of the problem for most men when he writes, "Men do not know who they are as men. They tend to define themselves by what they do, who they know, or what they own."[3]

Dalbey's words speak volumes of truth about men in today's culture. Many of us don't even know who we are, so we base our identity on what we do or who we know or the cool new toy we just bought. We try to craft our identity around those things — and we wind up feeling confused, empty, and deeply discouraged.

Unless you know who you really are, you'll struggle your whole life with feeling significant and important. Oh, I realize that many men walk around their homes with chests puffed out and eyes lifted high. They may be very accomplished at giving the appearance of feeling supremely important. Some call that arrogance, and, truth be told, men have a unique ability to act that way. Call it a gift.

But beneath the disguise — and that's all it is — deep within the hearts of most men lies a strong and unfulfilled desire to feel significant, important, special. Why unfulfilled? Because

> *Men . . . tend to define themselves by what they do, who they know, or what they own.*

it's a struggle for most men to know who they really are.

Don't kid yourself! Manhood is *not* easy; manhood is tough. The challenge is to avoid the many dead-ends that promise to fill your heart with significance. I can think of many such dead-ends, but I believe we fall prey to three in particular, each named in Dalbey's statement above. If you try to find your significance by traveling on any of these busy roads, sooner or later you will come to a dead-end every time . . . and leave traffic feeling unfulfilled and empty.

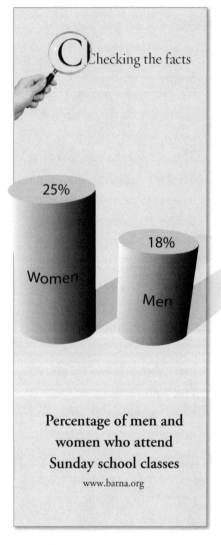

Checking the facts

25%

Women

18%

Men

Percentage of men and women who attend Sunday school classes

www.barna.org

Dead-end Road # 1: What You Do

What usually happens when men meet for the first time? What's the first thing they tend to say? Most men I know ask the same question: "So, what do you do?"

We men always want to describe what we do for a living. We feel good when we can tell others about our job, especially when we can let it slip about how well we're succeeding at it. And believe me, pastors are no different. We might try to cloak it a bit and make it sound *very* spiritual — "Yes, the Lord was good this year. We had 917 baptisms, praise be to God" — but it comes down to the same thing. We're trying to find a big chunk of our identity in what we do, and we think it doesn't hurt a bit to compare our performance with that of others.

But no man ever finds a sense of long-term peace simply through what he does. No matter how good he gets or what he accomplishes, it's never enough to fill the gaping hole inside. And what happens when he can no longer do the thing that he hoped would give him significance? What if you're a starting pitcher for the San Francisco Giants, let's say, and you suddenly lose your pitching arm to cancer? The question is more

> *. . . if you try to find your significance in what you do, you're headed for hard times.*

than theoretical to Dave Dravecky, who suffered exactly that fate. In his book, *The Worth of a Man*, Dravecky tells what happened to him emotionally and spiritually when, in the middle of his baseball career, he lost the ability to do the only thing he had ever wanted to do.[4]

Believe me, if you try to find your significance in what you do, you're headed for hard times. You might even end up a one-armed man in a two-armed world.

Dead-end Road #2: Who You Know

Have you noticed that men are sometimes the world's worst at name-dropping? They just can't seem to shake the habit.

"Oh yes, I know Shaquille. I was with him the other day."

And how well do you know him?

"Oh, we know each other *real* well."

Do you know his wife's name?

"Well, no. But we know each other real well."

We men tend to do silly things like this because we believe that some of the razzle-dazzle of the celebrity we "know" will rub off on us. And the truth is, sometimes people *do* seem impressed that we know so-and-so and therefore we *do* feel a surge of importance — but unfortunately, the impression soon fades and the feeling soon evaporates. And then we find ourselves all alone once again, wishing from the bottom of our hollow hearts that we felt better about who we really are.

There's a second serious problem with this one. What happens when *you're* the one who other men

> *No man has ever found long-term significance by who he knows.*

love to say they "know"? What happens when you're the celebrity or the star . . . and you know the truth, that fame costs more than it's worth and that you're no different from anyone else? Who can you "know" to give you a sense of identity? You've got nothing. And if you try to find your identity based on nothing, it'll tear your heart out.

No man has ever found long-term significance by who he knows. (Unless that someone is God. But let's not get ahead of ourselves! We'll get to that a little later.)

Dead-end Road #3: What You Own

This is the new tract in malehood today. Countless men are trying to gain significance by buying and owning stuff.

"Let me show you my new toy."

"You need to see this brand new piece of property I bought. It's amazing."

"Great car, huh?"

We go on and on about something we own. The problem is, the thing never really gives you the sense of significance you thought it would. It might create envy in the heart of the guy you show it to, but if you try to use envy as the foundation on which to build your skyscraper of significance, you had better get used to climbing out of a pile of stinking rubble. Significance is far too heavy a thing to be supported by something as rotten as envy.

"Stuff" just can't get the job done. The thrill it provides usually wears off long before it gets its first dent or suffers its first breakdown. I have a friend who, as a young man, pled with his parents to get him what he considered a cool stereo system. He badgered them for months, until finally, on his birthday, they gave it to him. He thoroughly enjoyed it . . . for a couple of weeks. And then he decided that this hissing eight-track contraption didn't give him the satisfaction he'd always assumed it would. And so for years it sat in his room, collecting dust, until one day it wound up in a thrift store.

Do you think that owning more stuff, or certain kinds of stuff, or new stuff, or antique stuff, or chrome-plated stuff, or diamond-encrusted stuff, or any kind of stuff at all, will give you the significance your heart craves? It won't. It can't. God never meant it to.

The Bible is our authority as Christian men, and the Bible never grants to men (or to women) *any* significance based on any of these three dead-end roads.

> *Do you think that owning more stuff . . . will give you the significance your heart craves?*

Travel them if you want to, but they won't lead anywhere other than to a gray, moldy wall at the end of a dark, dangerous alley.

If you want to find and enjoy true significance as a man, then leave behind the dead-end roads of this world and hop on God's freeway. And if you need a guide, I have just the guy in mind. He may not have written *the* book on the subject, but he certainly wrote *a* terrific book that's pointed me to no less than seven keys to male significance.

Interested? Then let's get going.

Endnotes

1 Survey conducted by Kenny Loveca of Every Man Ministries.

2 John Elliott and Zoe Brennan, "Stop Feeling Guilty: Lust Is Good for You," *The Sunday Times On Line*, www.timesonline.co.uk/article/0,,8122-960983,00.00.html

3 Gordon Dalbey, *Healing the Masculine Soul*: How God Restores Men to Real Manhood (Nashville, TN: Word Publishing Group, 2003).

4 Dave Dravecky, *The Worth of a Man* (Grand Rapids, MI: Zondervan, 1996).

Chapter 4

Seven Principles for Significance,

PART I

IF you want to know who you really are and how you can find true significance, I believe I can introduce you to a man who understood both things about as well as anyone in history. He didn't have an easy life, but he did have a tremendously significant one. And I suspect that by the end of his very productive life, he wouldn't have dreamed of trading significance for ease.

I'm talking about the Old Testament prophet Jeremiah.

We learn in the first chapter of Jeremiah's book that God shaped this boy into a true man's man. Although he lived a life full of conflict — God used him to announce coming judgment against

This man's man, this exemplar of masculinity, faced down physical threats, endured a trial for his life, landed in stocks for his faith, had to flee the authorities, got slandered by a false prophet, even was thrown into a deep pit. Yet he stayed faithful to God through it all. How? He didn't try to find his significance in what he owned, who he knew, or by what he did. He could remain faithful because he understood, both biblically and spiritually, what it means to feel and to be significant.

Judah, the people of God, and the people didn't much care for his message — he kept on going for more than five decades. At the time he dictated the first chapter of his book, he probably was no more than a college age kid, some 20 to 25 years of age. History records that he may have celebrated up to 90 birthdays.

God breathed into young Jeremiah's heart seven key principles that enabled him to stay strong even in very tough circumstances. These same seven principles can do exactly the same thing for you.

Principle #1: God Fashioned You

The word of the LORD came to me, saying, "Before I formed you in the womb I knew you" (Jer. 1:4–5).

Even before the prophet's birth, even before Jeremiah began to take shape in his mother's womb, God knew him. It's as if God said to him, "Before you were even a part of your mama's prayers and your daddy's dreams, I fashioned you."

Why did God tell Jeremiah this? What was so important about this piece of information? At the very beginning, God wanted Jeremiah to know that he was important and significant to the Lord — just like every man.

I can't overstate how crucial it is that you "get" this fact. You are important to God! You are significant to God! Before you even started taking shape in the womb of your mama, God — the Lord of heaven, the great and majestic God, full of grandeur and creativity — fashioned you, formed you, created you. And why did He take such care? Because you are important to Him.

This world may make you feel like dirt, but so what? You are important to God. Your wife or family

You are important to God!
You are significant to God!

may at times fail to make you feel significant. But you cannot get your significance even from your wife or kids. You *must* get your significance from God. And one part of His plan for personal significance is that He fashioned you.

You are the handiwork of God. You are God's masterpiece. Consider what David says to God in Psalm 139:13-14: "For you formed my inward parts; you covered me in my mother's womb. I will praise you, for I am fearfully and wonderfully made." David is not talking only about himself; he's talking about every man made in the image of God. You, too, are fearfully and wonderfully made. But David doesn't stop there.

"Marvelous are your works," he writes, "and that my soul knows very well." When David considers the meticulous care with which God fashioned him, he can't help but give accolades and praise to God. "My frame was not hidden from you when I was made in secret and skillfully wrought in the lowest parts of the earth," he continues. "Your eyes saw my substance being yet unformed and in your book they all were written, the days fashioned for me, when as yet there were none of them."

Wow! Do you ever walk around in a funk, wondering if God has forgotten you? Unfortunately, we all do it occasionally — but there really is no need to. The Psalmist reminds us of the marvelous, intimate, intricate work of God in giving substance to our unformed bodies. Does your own soul know this "very well"? The Psalmist's did, and the knowledge made a tremendous difference in the way he lived.

You're very special to God, a fact that all by itself

provides you with tremendous significance. And yet it doesn't stop there. God not only took special care in forming you in your mother's womb, He took equally great care in planning the course of your entire life. Just think of it: God had a plan for you even before you were born! Isn't that amazing? Maybe you thought you were an accident. Maybe you thought you were a mistake. But God had a plan for you even before you entered this world.

God doesn't take such meticulous care of things He deems unimportant. He doesn't spend so much energy on items that He considers insignificant. The Lord of the universe fashioned you, *you in particular*. Do you want to know who you are as a man? Then start by concentrating on what God has done in you as a marvelous work of His creation.

Principle #2: God Sanctified You

"Before you were born," God tells Jeremiah, "I sanctified you" (Jer. 1:5). The word "sanctified" means "set apart."

The Bible never even hints that a wife should serve as the spiritual leader of her home.

God set Jeremiah apart for His kingdom — and He sets you apart for the same thing. That means God has invested you with holy significance.

And for what have you been set apart? Let's talk about two of the most important things.

> *God has set us apart for male headship, for male leadership.*

First, you have been set apart for male headship of the family. Do you realize that God has destined you to be the head of your family? (1 Cor. 11:3; Eph. 5:23). The Bible never even hints that a wife should serve as the spiritual leader of her home. I believe that the only reason women gain headship authority in the home is because passive men yield it to them. Most wives will willingly step back if their husbands would just step up. I have never known a family to be all it can be with dominant women in control. That's not the way to bring up boys.

Second, men have been given headship in the church (1 Tim. 2:12). I thank God for the thousands of godly women who have kept hundreds of male-deficient churches afloat. But God's plan for the church calls for male headship; men are to lead in the body of Jesus Christ. That is God's will. God

has designed the church to become all it can be under male leadership. Female leadership will never create or sustain great churches. In fact, I've never known a church to become all that it needs to be under female leadership. That's simply not the way God meant it. It's just not the divine design. When a vacuum takes place in male leadership, female leadership rises to the surface. Now, I'm glad it does — but it is never God's intention. It is never God's best.

Does that mean women are insignificant? Does that mean women have no place of importance? Absolutely not! But I wrote this book to challenge men to step it up; balance will have to wait for another book.

It is time, men, that we step it up, first in our own personal headship in the family, and then in our personal headship in the church of Jesus Christ. God has set us apart for male headship, for male leadership. God has called us to be leaders. We have significance because God has set us apart for a purpose. We have been set apart for male headship and male leadership.

Principle #3:
God Chose You

God told Jeremiah, "I ordained you" (Jer. 1:5). The word "ordained" is simply another way to say,

"chosen." God is telling Jeremiah — and you and me — that He chose us.

Jesus had exactly this thought in His mind when He told His disciples, "You have not chosen me, but I have chosen you, and ordained you, that you would bear fruit and that your fruit should remain" (John 15:16).

God chose Jeremiah to be a prophet to the nations. He ordained him and set him apart to speak God's words both to Israel and to the surrounding kingdoms.

For what has God chosen you? Let me suggest three things.

First, God has chosen you for *purpose*. Since God has a purpose for you, you are to be a man of purpose. So let me ask you: What is your purpose? The ultimate purpose of every man is to live in such a way so as to bring glory and honor to God. Whatever

> *The ultimate purpose of every man is to live in such a way so as to bring glory and honor to God.*

you do, wherever you do it, you are to do it all for the honor and the glory of Jesus Christ (1 Cor. 10:31; Col. 3:17).

Second, God has chosen you for *witness*. Nothing compares to men taking on their calling as witnesses for Jesus Christ! Men can make a difference wherever they choose to do so. If you'll just step it up and say, "I will be a faithful witness for my Lord," you can make a huge difference all around you. No one can do this like a man. It's just amazing; it's part of male headship and leadership. When a man gets his heart on fire for God and begins to share his faith with others, he's able to witness even through his godly business ethics. He's able to point people to God through his business values. He's able to win people to Christ through his business testimony. What an incredible impact you can have, all across the world!

Third, you have been chosen for *the kingdom of God*. This is the big one; if you miss this one, you miss it all. This is not about *your* kingdom. I know too many men who have spent their lives building their own kingdoms. It's a dead-end road. So you build your kingdom; so what? What's another deal? What's another thousand dollars? What's another few shares of stock? It's all going to burn up.

> *Everything you do, you do for the ultimate purpose of using your resources and gifts and talents to expand God's kingdom.*

But what about the kingdom of God? That's a different story entirely. When you get to work on behalf of the kingdom of God, as Paul might say, "your labor is not in vain" (1 Cor. 15:58). And remember, you've been *chosen* for the kingdom, for just such a time as this. If you partner faithfully with God in His work of expanding the kingdom of God, those who come after you could say, just as it was said of King David, that you "served God's purpose in his own generation" (Acts 13:36). What is that but significance? Significance! What a blessing to know that God has chosen you, as a man, to make a difference for the kingdom of God. That's the kind of significance God wants you to have. That's what you're about.

Yes, you continue to work hard in the business world. Yes, you bust it to succeed. Yes, you make as much money as you can — but not for the ultimate purpose of accumulating wealth. Rather, you build as much as you can for the glory of God. Everything you do, you do for the ultimate purpose of using your resources and gifts and talents to expand God's kingdom throughout the world. That's what life is all about.

Does this sound like a tall order? It should! Because it really is. Jeremiah certainly thought so. When God gave the young prophet a peek into where his amazing career would

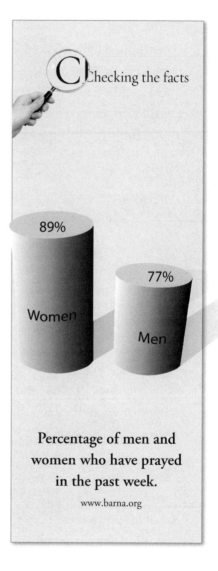

Checking the facts

89% Women

77% Men

Percentage of men and women who have prayed in the past week.

www.barna.org

take him, the intimidated young man told God he just couldn't do it. He wasn't up to the task. He

> *You don't need a college education or a seminary background before you can get busy.*

didn't have the right gifts or the right constitution. "Ah, LORD God!" Jeremiah objected. "Behold, I do not know how to speak, for I am only a youth" (Jer. 1:6). In other words, he complained, "God, I can't do that; look at me, I'm no orator. I never took forensics in school. And I didn't do well in speech class. I can't speak effectively in public.

Besides, I'm too young. I don't have the experience necessary for a job like this. I don't have the background. Who would listen to me even if I did speak?"

If you're a young man, or a teenager, or a young boy, let me say something specifically to you. Never let Satan tell you that you can't make a difference until you're 30 or 40 or 50. If you wait to try something for God until you're a middle-aged fat guy, you'll end up like a lot of men that age who have yet to make a difference for God because they waited. They're *still* waiting. Don't wind up like that. As a young man, I began preaching the Word at various little churches in my area. I'm sure I wasn't the best, but I gave it my best. Rest assured that God *wants* to use you and that God *will* use you. Just step out in faith.

"But will anybody listen to me?" you ask. It has nothing to do with whether anybody will listen to you. God has blessed you. God has a word for you — and when you share that word, you step up to the plate and become what God wants you to be. If you love Him when you're young, you'll love Him when you're old. If you serve Him when you're young, you'll serve Him when you're old. But if you wait and meander

in the meantime, all you'll ever be is one big bag of wind. Don't make such a foolish choice. Make a difference!

"Well, I don't know what I want to do," you say. Don't say it. God has called you to get out there and do something. What are you waiting on?

You don't need a college education or a seminary background before you can get busy. By all

Do you think that owning more stuff . . . will give you the significance your heart craves?

means, go after those things — but education doesn't qualify you to get busy for God. Some of the deadest preaching in the world comes from men with doctoral degrees. A Ph.D. doesn't qualify you for squat.

The best thing you can do with your life is to get where God wants you to be, *right now*. Learn to love Him; learn to walk with Him; and then stand and proclaim Him. Your youthfulness may cause you to do some things in a less-than-polished way — it did me — but let 'er rip anyway. God has a plan for you.

Like many men today, Jeremiah had several excuses why he couldn't serve God as a man's man. But unlike many men today, Jeremiah overcame those excuses. He grew beyond them. Do you know how he overcame them? Because he began to feel significant. When he finally saw himself as fashioned, set apart, and chosen, those old excuses began to break apart like a pistachio in a nutcracker. There's no reason for any man to spend his life making excuses why he can't serve God.

So — if the three truths Jeremiah just gave you don't yet float your boat, then get ready for another four. And if these don't give you a strong feeling of significance as a man, then I'm not sure what will.

True godliness leaves the
world, convinced beyond a
shadow of a doubt, that the
only explanation for you, is
Jesus Christ, to whose eternally
unchanging and altogether
adequate "I AM!" your
heart has learned to say with
unshatterable faith, "Thou art!"

—*W. Ian Thomas*

Chapter 5

Seven Principles for Significance, PART II

As a young man just starting out in his career, Jeremiah learned a surprising lesson. He discovered that God not only gave him particular words to say, He also gave him specific words *not* to say.

What were the forbidden words? If you didn't peek in your Bible, you probably wouldn't have guessed.

"Do not say, 'I am a youth,' " God commanded Jeremiah (Jer. 1:7).

The Lord forbade the prophet from ever using his age as an excuse for not stepping up like a man and serving God.

Let me say it as plainly as I can: Your age *never* matters to God. God can use you when you're young and God can use you when

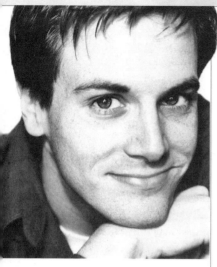

not too old to serve God. Your age *never* matters to God. You know why your age doesn't matter to God? The answer goes straight to the fourth reason that filled Jeremiah with great significance as a man.

Principle # 4: God Sent You

God told Jeremiah, "For you shall go to all to whom I send you and whatever I command you, you shall speak" (Jer. 1:7). A 20-something Jeremiah could serve as a prophet to his nation, not because his education brought him credibility, but because the authority of God sent him. *God* sent him; that's authority.

you're old. One group on the young side says, "I'm not sure I'm old enough." Some people agree with them and tell them so. And then some people on the other side are saying, "I'm too old, too tired, too worn out." And others agree with them and tell them so.

I have a word for both groups: get over it! You're not too young and you're

You, too, have been sent. If you're a believer in Christ, Jesus has said to you, "All authority in heaven and on earth has been given to me. Therefore go and make disciples of all nations, baptizing them in the name of the Father and of the Son and of the Holy Spirit, and teaching them to obey everything I have commanded you. And surely I am with you always, to the very end of the age" (Matt. 28:18–20).

God sent you. He has given you purpose and significance. He has called you and given you destiny. He has promised to help you. He will give you the message you need to speak at the very time you need to speak it (Matt. 10:19–20). God *will* use you. You just need to believe it.

How will He send you? I can't say for sure. He may be sending you around the world as a representative of a corporation. He may be sending you from the private business sector. He may be sending you as a volunteer or as a teacher or as a craftsman or as an advisor. But however He may send you, He does send you — so go with authority.

> *You're not too young and you're not too old to serve God. Your age never matters to God.*

May I ask you a question? Do you feel you have reached a point of destiny in your life? That's so important. Men have to feel that they are living out their destiny. If they don't, they feel miserable . . . and then they make everyone around them feel miserable.

I can personally testify to a feeling of destiny. I feel called and sent for just such a time as this. As I write, I have served as pastor of my current church for almost 20 years. Do you know, I feel just as destined and as sent today as I did almost two decades ago. In some ways, I feel it even more strongly. I am destined!

Do I always feel this sense of destiny? Do I always feel it as strongly? My life, like yours, has had its ups and downs. Life is a constant challenge — but there's never been a time when I haven't worked through the challenge to once again grasp that feeling of destiny. I feel it most when I know that God has sent me. Many times in my life certain opportunities or positions seemed good, but I didn't believe God was sending me there. God knows me better than I could ever know myself, and I thank God that I didn't end up in all the places I thought I needed to be. I would be one schizophrenic dude!

My wife, Jeana, and I sometimes visit little towns to attend football games and hang out a little. We drive by the First Baptist Church of Podunk, with a tiny old church parsonage about as big as a choir loft, and I tell her, "By the grace of God, that would be you and that would be me." Don't get me wrong; I don't mean that being the pastor of the First Baptist Church of Podunk isn't good — it emphatically *is* good — but do you know why it's good? It's good because that is where God sent that pastor. If God sends you there, it's good; if He doesn't, it isn't.

One day, not so long ago, God sent me there.

Then on another day, a little more recently, He sent me where I am today. To be frank, I would rather be sent here instead of there! But I had to be faithful in the least things before God gave me the most. And I felt just as sent there as I feel sent here.

I served my first full-time pastorate in Milford, Texas, a town of about 700 friendly people and three or four old grouches — and all of those old boys attended my church. Still, I'll never forget my wife telling me, "I could just live here all of my life." And she meant it with all of her heart! There is one good thing about being young: you're real dumb and you never know certain things. But it *was* good there. Why? Because God sent us there. We saw God move in powerful ways during

> *A man needs to feel he's sent. He wants to feel he's destined.*

our three years in Milford. Why? Because we were sent.

That's what all men need, the sure sense that God has sent them. Men want to feel they're destined. So don't let anyone hold you back from it! Instead, fan the flames of your destiny. Look for people to support you in the midst of discovering your unique destiny.

May I ask you, do you feel sent? Do you feel destined? Do you feel like Jeremiah must have felt? Can you say, "God has chosen me for this moment and this time in history. I'm doing what God has called me to do and I'm keeping my eyes on the kingdom the whole time."

Nothing is like the touch of God. You and I need a divine touch from God to feel a deep sense of destiny.

A man has to know, "this is for me." A man needs to feel he's sent. He wants to feel he's destined. Do you need to feel this sense of being sent, this sense of destiny, again? Maybe right now, you don't feel it. That's why you must have the next thing Jeremiah discovered — it will help you get through whatever trouble you might be in right now.

Principle #5: God Touched You

Jeremiah had a remarkable experience, described in Jeremiah 1:9: "Then the LORD put forth His hand and touched my mouth."

What a moment that must have been! The Lord put His hand on this young man and touched his lips. Wow! Isn't that exactly what each one of us needs?

Well, I have some great news for you. God *wants* to touch you. He *wants* to put forth His hand on you, to touch your mouth, and to say to you, "Behold your purpose." And when that happens, the light goes on: you glimpse your destiny! The light goes on again: you understand and feel your significance!

Nothing is like the touch of God. You and I need a divine touch from God to feel a deep sense of destiny. I don't completely understand what it is or how it happens, but I can tell you that I know it when it takes place. I've been there. I've lived it. I've begged God for that touch again. There's something amazing, even breathtaking, about it.

Author John Piper wrote about God's touch in a way I'll never forget. In a profound meditation based on 1 Samuel 10:26 — "Saul also went to his house at Gibeah; and the valiant men whose hearts God had touched went with him" — Piper said:

> The touch of God is an awesome thing because God is God. Just think of what is being said here! God touched them. Not a wife. Not a child. Not a parent. Not a counselor. But God. The One with infinite power in the universe. The One with infinite authority, infinite wisdom, infinite love,

infinite goodness, infinite purity, and infinite justice. That One touched their hearts. How does the circumference of Jupiter touch the edge of a molecule, let alone penetrate to its nucleus?

The touch of God is awesome because it is a touch. It is a real connection. . . . The valiant men were not just spoken to. They were not just swayed by a divine influence. They were not just seen and known from outside. God, with infinite condescension, touched their hearts. God was that close. And they were not consumed.

I love that touch. I want it more and more. . . . I pray that God would touch me and all his church in a new, deep way for his glory. . . . O that the saints of God would be valiant for the Lord — courageous and mighty and full of weighty truth and beauty!

Pray with me for that touch. If it comes with fire, so be it. If it comes with water, so be it. If it comes with wind, let it come,

O God. If it comes with thunder and lightning, let us bow before it. O Lord, come. Come close enough to touch. Shield us with the asbestos of grace, but no more. Pass through all the way to the heart, and touch. Burn and soak and blow and crash. Or, in a still, small voice. Whatever the means, come. Come all the way and touch our hearts.[1]

The touch of God determines the destiny of a man as well as his sense of that destiny. Every unmarried young woman looking for a husband needs to find a young man who understands and craves the touch of God. He may look rough on the outside, but one who knows the touch of God will be far better in the long run than the guy who looks like a hunk but has no clue regarding the true meaning and purpose of life.

> *The touch of God determines the destiny of a man as well as his sense of that destiny.*

Have you experienced the touch of God? Do you want to? Would you like to be a "valiant man whose heart God touched"? If so, you can do something about it. You can begin to pray, right now, that God would touch you. Whether it comes with fire or water or wind or thunder and lightning, pray for it. And

> *Don't ever get over the miracle that the Lord uses you!*

when it comes, thank God for it — and then step out in faith and do whatever God has sent you to do. As a real man.

Principle #6: God Uses You

The Lord told Jeremiah that He intended to use the prophet in several ways. For one thing, He planned to use Jeremiah as His mouthpiece: "Whatever I command you, you shall speak" (Jer. 1:7) and "behold, I have put my words in your mouth" (Jer. 1:9).

For another thing, He intended to use Jeremiah in a way that put those words into mighty action: "I have this day set you over the nations, over the kingdoms, to root out and to pull down, to destroy and to throw down, to build and to plant" (Jer. 1:10).

God wants to use you every bit as much as He used Jeremiah. He wants to use you not only as a willing servant (Eph. 6:7), but as a fellow worker, a partner (1 Cor. 3:9; 2 Cor. 6:1). Don't ever get over the miracle that the Lord uses you! Just think of it: why should He ever use *you*?

"Well, I'm a pretty good guy," you say. "I have a lot of great gifts."

Oh, please. Don't you think there are people all around the world who have more talent, more experience, more energy, more skills, and more focus than you? God doesn't use you because He just can't get along without you. A needy God wouldn't say, "I have no need of a bull from your stall or of goats from your pens, for every animal of the forest is mine, and the cattle on a thousand hills. I know every bird in the mountains, and the creatures of the field are mine. If I were hungry I would not tell you, for the world

is mine, and all that is in it" (Ps. 50:9–12). A needy God would not inspire words like the following from His choicest servants: "The God who made the world and everything in it is the Lord of heaven and earth and does not live in temples built by hands. And he is not served by human hands, as if he needed anything, because he himself gives all men life and breath and everything else" (Acts 17:24–25).

So why does God use you? He uses you because it pleases Him to use you. It gives Him joy to partner with you in the building of His kingdom. In other words, He chooses you out of sheer grace. You don't earn the privilege, you don't deserve it, and you don't impress God by your willingness to be used. Does a master craftsman thank the tool he made when he uses that tool to create a beautiful piece of art? Of course not. But if that tool could talk, I'll bet it would wear itself out thanking the craftsman for creating it for his use in making the world a more beautiful place.

God uses you! Sometimes He uses you to do easy things and sometimes He uses you to do hard things. I've been in

churches where I've had to root out and pull down. I've had to destroy and I have had to throw away. I've also had to build and I've had to plant. But in every case, it was God using me for His purposes.

How will God use you? In what way will He do it? He will do it in the same way He did it in Jeremiah's life.

First, God will give you a word. Many years ago I visited a church to see if it might be a good "fit" for me. I wasn't quite sure if I needed to be there. Church officials kept my family and me in two rooms; my family went to one room while I knelt down by a bed in another. On that hot,

humid Texas afternoon, I said, "God, I need to know that You want me here. I can tell this wouldn't be

> *He knew he had been sent. He knew God had touched his life.*

easy here; I know it. It's been fun where I've been, and if you send me back there, praise God, I'll roll. But if you want me here, I have to have a word from you."

You know what God gave me? Jeremiah 1.

A little over a month ago one of the "preacher boys" from our church, who I love like a son, had to go through a bump in his ministry. He had to fire a staff member. A shaking came, and although Brad's just a very young man, God sent him and is using him. Early one morning when I was praying for him, God prompted me to pray Jeremiah 1 over him. I wrote him an e-mail: "Brad, this is God's word for you today, Jeremiah 1."

God has given you authority over all of your enemies and over everything in your life — so claim your ground

Now he's through the worst of it. He's making it. God is winning, people are getting saved, and the church is growing — Brad just had to get a bunch of old, dead weeds out of the way. He did it with authority. How? He had a word from God. I'm so proud of him! He was willing to act courageously when he could have compromised his life and his message. But he didn't do that. Why not? He knew he had been sent. He knew God had touched his life. And he knew God wanted to use him.

Second, God will position you for maximum use capacity. You want to hear some great news? Here it is: *You already are where God wants to use you.* Too many people I know go running here and running there, wondering where

God wants to use them. You know what? You don't have to run around, always wanting to be somewhere else. Get usable where you already are, and God will wear you out.

Third, God will use you in multiple ways, far beyond anything you can imagine. Don't limit God the way we sometimes try to do. We say, "I'm *sure* He's going to use me in this particular way." Well, maybe He will; then again, maybe He won't. He may choose to use you in ways that have never occurred to you. That's why God told Jeremiah, "I'm going to use you — but I'll use you in the way I see fit. Sometimes I'm going to let you root something out, pull it down, destroy it. At other times I'm going to let you build and let you plant. The good news is that I've equipped you to do whatever I want you to do. So be a man, and go and do it."

God wants to use you. And you're well equipped for His use, because you are fashioned, set apart, chosen, sent, and touched — you're a man of destiny! So go claim your Canaan. And go after it with all that God has given you.

Principle # 7: God Is With You

If you haven't yet gotten a feel for the significance God wants you to sense as a man, get ready for the last and greatest discovery Jeremiah made. The prophet found out, as others had before him and after him, that God was with him.

There is nothing like knowing that God is with you. *Nothing.* And God *is* with you! God told Jeremiah, "Do not be afraid of their faces" (Jer. 1:8). Why would the Lord tell him such a thing? " 'For I

> *. . . rise and take hold of your destiny, for sovereign choice determines sovereign destiny.*

am with you to deliver you,' says the LORD."

I'll admit that I've been afraid of the faces of some church members. But God tells me I don't have to be afraid. Why not? Because

He has promised to be with me.

That doesn't mean that opposition won't come! Jeremiah knew better. God himself told him so: "They will fight against you" (Jer. 1:19). Oh yes, they will. Sometimes they come in waves. But notice the very next verse: "But they shall not prevail against you." Just because they huff and puff and want to blow your house down, doesn't mean they are capable of doing it. God has given you power to walk upon the scorpions of the world (Luke 10:19). God has given you power to shake and rattle the gates of hell (Matt. 16:18). God has given you authority over all of your enemies and over everything in your life — so claim your ground (Matt. 9:8; 10:1; 2 Cor. 10:8; Titus 2:15; Rev. 2:26).

Take special note of what God says in that last phrase: "For I am with you to deliver you." God is with us not only as a guide. He's not with us only as a companion. He's not with us only as a counselor. He is with us as a deliverer. I don't know about you, but I need that assurance in my life. God is telling you and me that we have no reason to fear. As a man, what do you fear? Most of us fear failure more than anything else. But God declares that He is here, with us, ready and able and eager to deliver us.

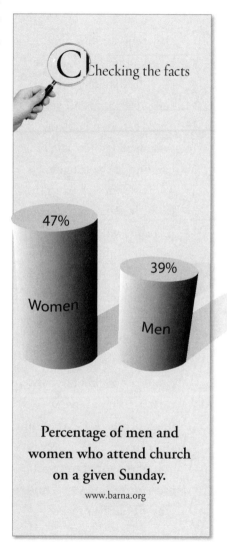

Checking the facts

47% Women

39% Men

Percentage of men and women who attend church on a given Sunday.

www.barna.org

Jeremiah not only heard about God's deliverance, he experienced it, time after time and year after year. It amazes me that although Jeremiah had one of the toughest ministries described in the Bible, he nevertheless lived to a ripe, old age. Even though conflict — serious conflict, harsh conflict, life-threatening conflict — constantly filled his life, God let Jeremiah live to be an old man. Maybe the prophet should had known he was going to live so long, because God told him right in verse 19, "They're going to fight against you, but you will prevail." And why would he prevail?

Because the Lord promised to be with him.

God has made you the same promise. The writer of Hebrews tells us:

> God has said,
>
> > "Never will I leave you; never will I forsake you."
>
> > So we say with confidence,
>
> > "The Lord is my helper; I will not be afraid.
> > What can man do to me?" (Heb. 13:5–6).

Would you like to hear some wonderful news? Men who belong to God are *never* alone. Let me tell you something else that should make you shout. Write this one down on the whiteboard of your mind:

> *Sovereign choice leads to sovereign purpose and sovereign purpose leads to sovereign protection.*

When you realize that you are chosen by a sovereign God to be where you are for such a time as this, you have purpose. It doesn't matter whether you're a preacher or a businessman or a teacher or a factory worker or a mailman or a soldier. Something about sovereign purpose leads you to feel protected. Of course, that's not an invitation to be stupid — but never forget that because God is with you, you're protected.

Get out of my way, man! I am a man of destiny. And so are you. So rise and take hold of your destiny, for sovereign choice determines sovereign destiny.

Endnotes

1. John Piper, *A Godward Life* (Sisters, OR: Multnomah Publishers, 1997), p. 79–80.

Astronaut Michael Collins, speaking at a banquet, quoted the estimate that the average man speaks 25,000 words a day and the average woman 30,000. Then he added: "Unfortunately, when I come home each day I've spoken my 25,000 — and my wife hasn't started her 30,000."

Chapter 6

Wanted: Battlefield Commanders

A reporter once asked Bill Parcells, the head coach of the NFL's Dallas Cowboys, "What do you want out of your quarterback?" I love his reply:

> "I want a battlefield commander."

That is exactly what we need quarterbacking the families of 21st century America. We need battlefield commanders working in the business world, working in the corporate world, serving people in their communities, leading their families. Teenage boys need to become this kind of man at their schools. We need battlefield commanders willing to model and illustrate what it means to be a man of strength.

More than ever, we need men who see themselves as battlefield commanders. Why?

Because we are in a war (1 John 2:16).

We are in a war with the flesh — *your* flesh. It's a tough enemy, and many of us are losing that war.

We're in a war with the world, but many of us have sold out to the ungodly system of our affluent, God-denying culture.

And we are in a war with Satan. Many men who sit in church, Sunday after Sunday, speak of freedom even as they remain in chains. They've become willing captives to the enemy.

We need battlefield commanders because we have to win this war. We serve a Commander-in-chief who has the firepower to bring us victory, if only we will follow His orders and keep open our supply lines. We need to be battlefield commanders in our homes and we need to be battlefield commanders in our communities. And we need to be characterized by at least three things.

1. Visionary men

As battlefield commanders, we need to become men of vision. Jesus was a man of vision. We need to see Jesus as the captain of our army (Josh. 5). And we need to see ourselves as battlefield commanders who go every day to the Commander-in-chief for our daily instructions. We *must* have that vision.

I challenge you today to see yourself as a warrior. That's what God wants you to be. You say, "But that's not me." No, it *is* you; that is how God made you. That is what it means to be a man.

The relationship of a man with Christ is more than a simple friendship; it is a rollicking adventure with Jesus. It is an exciting journey, a new territory to conquer. It is a mountain, and men love mountains. So come on, pack your gear, join me, and let's climb that summit for God.

2. Deliberate men

A battlefield commander is deliberate. We need to be deliberate in our adventure with Christ. We must be deliberate in rearing our children and

> *The relationship of a man with Christ is more than a simple friendship; it is a rollicking adventure with Jesus.*

grand children. We must be deliberate in our relationship with our wives and deliberate in our strategy of how best to be a man.

Let me say it like this: God wants you to be as deliberate in your walk with God as you are deliberate about your job, your career, your hobby, your favorite pastime, or whatever it is that you most love.

Are you deliberate?

Some men doubt a solid spiritual life is worth it, so they never put anything into it. And in life, you get what you prepare for. I believe that most Christian men *want* to become true men of God. They really do. But most of us have a real issue with failure. We worry, "But what if I fail?" Well, you're going to fail

some. I fail every day. I make more mistakes than I can count. As a pastor, I don't get up in the pulpit Sunday by Sunday because I'm perfect; I get up there by grace. I am saved, not because of my works, but because of the gift of God. I don't get up to preach because I'm some great authority; I get up because a gracious God looks past my faults and chooses to use me periodically.

Would God use me even if I weren't deliberate about what I do and what I say? Perhaps; He's a gracious God, after all. But a battlefield commander has to be deliberate. A battlefield commander has no choice but to think ahead of time about how many troops he needs, where those soldiers need to go, what they have to do when they get there, and how to respond to the most likely enemy troop movements. Jesus himself encouraged us to think like battlefield commanders:

> . . . suppose a king is about to go to war against another king. Will he not first sit down and consider whether he is able with ten thousand men to oppose the one coming against him with twenty thousand? If he is not able, he will send a delegation while the other is still a long way off and will ask for terms of peace. In the same way, any of you who does not

give up everything
he has cannot
be my disciple
(Luke 14:31–33).

A battlefield commander deliberately gives up everything he has in order to accomplish his mission. Jesus calls us to do exactly the same thing.

3. Committed men

I hate to say it, but we have too many weak men today. We have too many men afraid to make a commitment. When you ask the typical male to commit to this or that endeavor, you're likely to hear, "Well, I don't know."

What do you mean you don't know?

"Well, I'm not sure."

What do you mean you're not sure? You're a man; surely you can be sure about it.

"Well, I need to be cautious here."

Stop being afraid! You need to step it up. And you need to commit to some-

We have too many men afraid to make a commitment.

thing important, something lasting, and something that blesses God's own heart. You need to commit to the thing God has called you to and touched you for and sent you to do.

"Commit" is not a nasty word. At the football stadium the other night, I

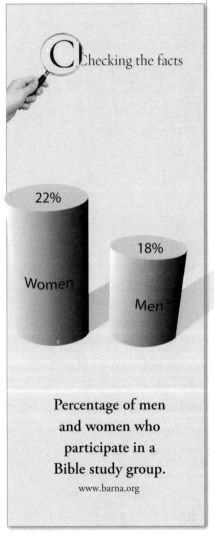

Checking the facts

22%

18%

Women

Men

Percentage of men and women who participate in a Bible study group.

www.barna.org

saw 70,000 people make a commitment, and I enjoyed every minute of it. I just pray that sometime in my life I'll see a group of men who will be just as committed to Christ and to His church as they are to their favorite sports team.

Why are men so afraid of commitment? Are they worried that it will cost them something? If that's your problem, you can stop worrying right now; it *will* cost you. Jesus says to you, "Anyone who does not carry his cross and follow me cannot be my disciple" (Luke 14:27). No one carries a cross unless he's going to die. We have to be willing to die. That's why the Book of Revelation applauds believers who "did not love their lives so much as to shrink from death" (Rev. 12:11).

Do you shrink from death? Do you fear a real and manly commitment to Christ? If so, don't be afraid to admit it. But pray for the courage to step it up. Pray for the boldness to overcome your fear. Courage isn't the absence of fear, but the willingness to push ahead even when your heart melts and your knees buckle.

A man's man has to be willing to die. He has to be willing to step it up. And that's exactly what God asks us as men to do, to make a promise to follow Him wholeheartedly — even if our hearts still feel a flutter or two of fear.

Part of our problem is that we don't understand a crucial, biblical word: "covenant." We don't

> *Courage isn't the absence of fear, but the willingness to push ahead even when your heart melts and your knees buckle.*

understand what it is to make a covenant with God. A covenant is a binding agreement between two parties, and it is a central feature of both the Old and the New Testaments.

May I suggest that God is calling you into a covenant today? He's calling you to make a covenant regarding your masculinity. He's asking you to commit to becoming a battlefield commander as a young boy, as a teenager, as a single adult, as a married man, even as a widower. God wants you to be a battlefield commander.

You and I are in a war with the flesh, the world, and with Satan. I do not want to lose this war; I want to win. Therefore, I commit to be a battlefield commander in my family, in my church, and in my community. I commit to demonstrate true, strong, biblical masculinity. I commit to consult with my Commander-in-chief, Jesus Christ, every day for my instructions. I commit to become as deliberate in my Christian faith as I am deliberate in everything else I love. I commit to becoming the spiritual leader God wants me to be in my family, in my community, and in my church. I commit to equip myself to become the best battlefield commander I can be. I commit my life and all God has given me to bring glory to God. Unashamedly, I commit to be "a warrior for the Lord," a battlefield commander for Christ, so help me God.

Ancient history teaches us that when Roman soldiers gave their military oath, they pledged to obey their commander and not to desert his standard. In the early Church, the Lord's Supper took on some war-related connotations; communion presented an opportunity for the soldiers of the Lord to reenlist in God's army.

Before I ask you to reenlist in God's army, I want to remind you of something. When Rome's soldiers took their oath, they pledged themselves to dying submission to their commander, to do as he wished, even to death. Our Commander-in-chief, Jesus Christ, expects nothing less from you. He asks that you live for Him, but He also asks that you lift His standard high above everything else. His standard is His cross. It is our banner, our call to death and our call to life. When you reenlist, you're holding up the Cross as your absolute standard of loyalty to Jesus Christ.

Whether you're a young boy or a senior adult man, single or married, I want to challenge you to seriously consider going into this covenant with me. Oh, it's a strong covenant! But I'm going to ask you to cut that covenant with God. It's between you and God, no one else. If you're willing, read it out loud and then, on the line below, write the date that you entered this covenant:

> *He also asks that you lift His standard high above everything else. His standard is His cross.*

COVENANT

I am at war. It is a war with the flesh, with the world and with Satan. I do not want to lose this war; I want to win. Therefore, I commit to be a battlefield commander in my family and in my community. I commit to demonstrate truth, strong biblical masculinity in my family and in my culture. I commit to consult my Commander-in-chief, Jesus Christ, every day for my instructions. I commit to become as deliberate in my Christian faith as I am deliberate in everything else I love. I commit to become the spiritual leader God wants me to be in my family, in my community, and in my church. I commit to get equipped to be the best battlefield commander I can be with the gifts God has given to me. I commit my life and all that God has given me to bring glory to God. I am an unashamed warrior for the lord, a battlefield commander for Christ, so help me God. The Lord is with me. Amen.

_____   _____
Your signature   Today's date

If you just entered this covenant with God, let me say that it's an honor to serve with you in the army of the Lord of glory. And let me leave you with the words of another battlefield commander, a man's man who overcame his fear to slay giants and take possession of the rich land that the Lord had given him:

Now fear the LORD and serve him with all faithfulness. Throw away the gods your forefathers worshiped beyond the River and in Egypt, and serve the LORD. But if serving the LORD seems undesirable to you, then choose for yourselves this day whom you will serve, whether the gods your forefathers served beyond the River, or the gods of the Amorites, in whose land you are living. But as for me and my household, we will serve the LORD.

– Josh. 24:14–15

PHOTO CREDITS

Also by Dr. Ronnie Floyd . . .

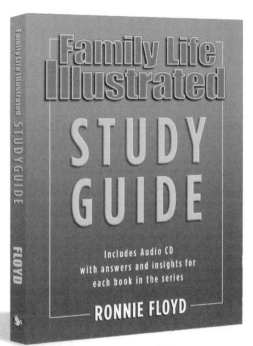

ISBN 0-89221-599-2

<u>Special Features Include:</u>
- Study questions in each book for reflection and to aid
  small-group study
- Study guide that works for all six books that also includes
  an audio CD from Dr. Floyd with answers and insights for
  each book.

5 1/4 x 8 3/8 • Paper • 128 pages
• *INCLUDES AUDIO CD*

Available at Christian bookstores nationwide.

Also by Dr. Ronnie Floyd . . .

ISBN 0-89221-588-7

Your job, your finances, your friends – nothing you ever do will matter as much as being a good parent to your child. Going beyond the surface strategies and quick psychobabble solutions, this book reveals solid, God-based insight on becoming a more effective parent. Don't choose to struggle alone — tap into the wealth of wisdom God wants to share with you and find how you can make a positive, remarkable, and lasting change in the lives of your children today!

Thought about your marriage lately? Or do you just take it for granted? Marriage is not a passive enterprise – it takes skill, work, and attention if you want it to survive in the "disposable" culture of our society today. Do you have the marriage God wants you to have? Tired of going through the motions, feeling helpless to make the change for the better you know you need to make? It's time to take control and make your marriage be the true partnership that God designed. Don't wait to make a renewed commitment for marital success!

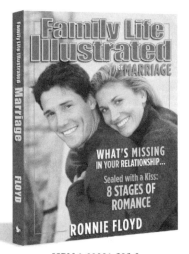

ISBN 0-89221-585-2

Available at Christian bookstores nationwide.

Also by Dr. Ronnie Floyd . . .

Are you happening to life or is life simply happening to you? Overwhelmed, overworked, stressed, and tired, it's easy to lose sight of things important to you as a woman, wife, and perhaps even a mother. Be empowered, be decisive, and be open to God's gently guiding hand in your life! God can be what you need – He can strengthen, calm, and sustain you when life seems impossible. No matter what you face, God can give you the knowledge and wisdom to adapt, endure, and affect a change!

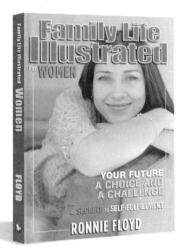

ISBN 0-89221-583-6

It seems like everything keeps changing and no one understands. Every day seems to bring more pivotal decisions to be made. Life is complicated and stressful, and you feel you are alone! Fight the isolation – don't be a spectator in your own life! Get powerful solutions and strategies to survive and thrive during the toughest time of your life – and find out how to rely on God when life overwhelms you!

ISBN 0-89221-586-0

Available at Christian bookstores nationwide.

Also by Dr. Ronnie Floyd . . .

ISBN 0-89221-587-9

Money, debt, credit card complications — believe it or not, the Bible can be the most practical guide to financial management you will ever find! Simple, easy-to-implement solutions don't require high cost solutions or painful personal concessions. Don't do without the answers which can help change your financial future and solve a critical area of stress affecting you, your family, or even your marriage. Invest in God's wisdom, and reap the blessings He has in store for you!

The Gay Agenda is a compelling and compassionate look at one of the most turbulent issues of our society today – homosexuality and same-sex marriage. Dr. Ronnie Floyd states the importance of maintaining the traditional family, while revealing the homosexual agenda at work in our schools, churches, and government. He also looks at the ongoing controversies over gay clergy, and turns the spotlight on judicial activism as well. Dr. Floyd makes clear the political chaos and confusion of this election-year hot potato as both major parties seek to find political payoffs on these issues. *The Gay Agenda* cannot be ignored.

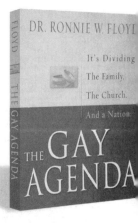

ISBN: 0-89221-582-8

7 x 9 • Casebound • 140 pages

Available at Christian bookstores nationwide.

About the Author . . .

Recognizing the vital importance of the family in the success of not only individuals, but for our society to-day, the "Family Life Illustrated" series offers real answers for real-life problems being faced each day by families. Articulate, informative, and always relevant — Dr. Ronnie Floyd is reaching the hearts of millions weekly through his broadcast ministry Invitation to Life, aired on WGN's Superstation and other television networks nationally each week. An accomplished author of 17 books as well as a powerful group speaker, Dr. Floyd has over 27 years of ministry experience and is senior pastor for a congregation of 15,000 in Northwest Arkansas. Dr. Floyd has been been seen on Fox News, WorldNetDaily, Janet Parshall's America, Washington Watch, USA Radio Network, FamilyNet, and more!

MORE RESOURCES FROM
DR. RONNIE W. FLOYD

CD/VHS/DVD
"Family Life Illustrated Series"

CD/VHS/DVD
"The Gay Agenda"

Other Books By Dr. Floyd
Life on Fire
How to Pray
The Power of Prayer and Fasting
The Meaning of a Man

Weekly International Television and Internet

Sundays: (7:30 a.m. CST) WGN SUPERSTATION

Thursdays: (9:00 p.m. CST) Daystar Christian Television Network

Sundays: (9:15 a.m. CST) Live webcast on
www.fbcspringdale.org

For more information on all resources: www.invitationtolife.org

For information about our church:
www.fbcspringdale.org   www.churchph.com

or call (479) 751-4523 and ask for Invitation to Life